Cannibals: Do people taste like chicken?

MARLA BUCHANAN

ISBN-10: 1500377910
ISBN-13: 978-1500377915

Cannibalism is when human beings eat the flesh or internal organs of other humans. A person who does this is called a *cannibal.*

Cannibalism was a common practice in the past in many parts of the world, continuing into the 19th century in some isolated cultures in the South Pacific, who called human 'meat,' "long-pig," and to the present day in parts of tropical Africa.

Leonhard Kern Menschenfresserian White

Munster cannibals

Cannibalism has been well documented around the world, from the Maori people in New Zealand to New Guinea and West (and central) Africa.

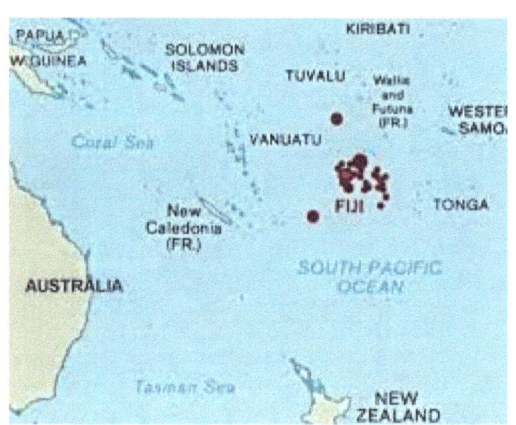

The South Pacific

Dutch cyclist Johannes Maas with cannibals in New Guinea, 1972

Some other areas that had cannibals were the Solomon Islands, some of the islands in Polynesia, Sumatra, Fiji, Europe, South America and the Iroquoian peoples of North America.

Mother and child cannibals in Borneo

Cannibal trophy skull from Borneo

Evidence of cannibalism has also been found in ruins associated with North American Anasazi culture. All South Sea islanders were once cannibals.

Some scientists believe that *Neanderthals* (an extinct species of human) might have been cannibals. It is also believed by some that physically-modern humans may have also eaten Neanderthals.

Neanderthals

A large number of butchered human bones have been found in Lower to Middle *Paleolithic* (stone-age) Neanderthal (and other) sites.

Cannibalism may have also occurred at that time due to *predation* (animals hunting other animals, including humans, for food) because the traditions of burying and burning of dead people came later.

Dead people might also have been eaten as a way to dispose of their bodies and keep hungry animals away from the living. They may also have been cannibalistic due to nutritional reasons. Humans eventually developed more advanced hunting techniques in order to prey on animals.

Other reasons for cannibalism include *cultural norms* (what is "normal" and accepted in a society); the belief that eating a person would give you their characteristics, and as a way of guiding the souls of the dead into the bodies of their living descendants.

Cannibals in South America

Russian famine, 1921, peasants with cannibalized bodies

Some people have resorted to cannibalism during desperate times, including periods of *famine* (extreme food shortage), as well as those being criminal acts and war crimes throughout the 20th and 21st century. Cannibalism was also a ritual practice in times of *drought* (long time without rain).

There was also a practice known as the "*custom of the sea*," which was when shipwrecked survivors would draw lots to see who would be killed and eaten so that the others might survive.

Serial killer and cannibal Albert Fish

Serial killer and cannibal Jeffery Dahmer, High School photo

Some mentally-ill people have obsessions about eating people and actually do so. There have been *serial killers* (people who kill certain groups of others on a regular basis) who have eaten their victims.

Interestingly enough, cannibalism isn't against the law in the U.S. and most European countries. Most criminals who commit acts of cannibalism are charged with murder or desecration of a corpse.

There have also been those who simply find people delicious to eat. They practice cannibalism because they enjoy it; they have *psychopathic* (an ongoing mental disorder with abnormal or violent social behavior) personalities, and they are extremely lonely. "Lonely" cannibals often believe that their consumption of the dead gives them control and a way to keep others with them forever.

Most cannibals are not *psychotic* (people who don't live in reality) and are well aware of what they are doing. It might be hard to believe, but most cannibals really aren't "crazy"—especially those who practice cannibalism due to cultural reasons.

"meat"

What does human "meat" taste like? I believe that most people have wondered about this at some time or another, especially after hearing about acts of cannibalism or the capture of one who has been accused of practicing it.

Just like any animal, the taste of a human is probably influenced by their daily diet—like milk-fed veal and corn-fed beef. People in Nordic countries who eat a lot of dairy products probably taste more veal-like.

In fact, cannibals have said that human flesh tastes like something between pork and veal, which it also resembles in appearance, texture and smell. The smell of burning human muscle tissue is said to resemble that of beef cooking in a frying pan.

Grilled "meat"

The smell of burning human body fat supposedly smells like a side of fatty pork on the grill. People that work in *crematoriums* (places that cremate the dead), especially near the *cremators* (furnaces used to cremate a dead body) say that it smells like burnt pork roast.

Some people have even sold it to an unsuspecting public. There was a German cannibal who was caught after he sold pickled human meat in jars that he had said contained pork. He had sold many jars before finally being caught.

There have also been accounts of firefighters that cannot stand to be around cooking pork because it reminds them of the smell of burning human flesh. In short, we probably taste like pork, "the other white meat."

Kuru is the human equivalent to mad cow disease which affects the brain and nervous system. Consuming animal or human flesh that contains an infected protein or *prion* causes brain deterioration, loss of motion control and eventually death.

Kuru is a *neurological* (nervous system) disorder that is *endemic* (regularly found among a certain people or particular area) to tribal regions of Papua New Guinea. The term "kuru" derives from the Fore word "kuria/guria" ("to shake") which is a reference to the body tremors that are a common symptom of the disease.

It is also known as the "laughing sickness" due to *pathological* (something caused by a physical or mental disease) bursts of laughter that people also display while afflicted with the disease.

It is now widely accepted that Kuru is transmitted via cannibalism

"Beef" stew

Now that you know all about cannibals and cannibalism you won't have to guess about what that (often) nasty-looking stew tastes like while watching your next horror movie featuring mutant, backwoods types. 'Cannibal's stew' is mmm, mmm good!—*at least to cannibals, anyway.*

"As your mother tells you, and my mother certainly told me, it is important, she always used to say, always to try new things." - Hannibal Lecter

Word-of-mouth is crucial for any author to succeed. If you enjoyed the book, please leave a review on Amazon. Even if it's just a sentence or two. It would make all the difference and would be very much appreciated.

Thank you.

ABOUT THE AUTHOR

Marla Buchanan is the author of the memoir, **Rescue in Arabia: a true story of abduction, tragedy and hope**, and the **Mulberry May Belle** children's book series. She is "happily on the doorstep of AARP membership," and a mother of four adult children (and the grandmother of one). She lives in Northern Illinois, and has worked in social services and education. She was married to her Syrian-born ex-husband, Salim Kassem, the father/abductor of their son, Mohamad ("Moe") Kassem, for approximately 6-1/2 years. They were divorced in 1994.

In October 2002, Moe was abducted by his father and taken to the Middle-East, where they remained until Salim was killed in a car-rollover in Saudi Arabia, in August 2007. Moe was left critically brain-injured and in a coma. Saudi Prince Muhammad bin Naïf bin Abdul-Aziz Al-Saud, the current Minister of the Interior, and nephew of King Abdullah, personally sponsored Moe's medical care and Marla's travel to, and stay in Saudi Arabia.

A college graduate, she earned her B.A. in Anthropology (Minor: Women's Studies) at Northern Illinois University, in DeKalb, Illinois, in May 2007, nearly 24 years after obtaining her G.E.D. She was a featured speaker during Women's History Month, at NIU, in March 2007, where she spoke about Moe's abduction, and was also named an "Outstanding Female Student of the Year."

Marla has traveled extensively throughout the Middle-East and Europe, visiting such countries as Syria, Jordan and Saudi Arabia, as well as England, Switzerland and Italy. She's also a 10-year cancer survivor after having been successfully treated for Papillary Thyroid Cancer in 2004. Recently diagnosed with the genetic movement disorder, Essential Tremor (ET) the author is determined to overcome this most recent challenge via her amazing ability to adapt and change. Her life is an evolutionary work in progress.

(Memoir/4.8 stars) **"Rescue in Arabia: a true story of abduction, tragedy and hope"**

On Saturday, October 12, 2002, 14 year-old Mohamad ("Moe") Kassem was abducted by his Syrian-born father and taken to the Middle-East. In August 2007, his father/abductor was killed along with his step-mother and youngest half-brother, in a car-rollover near Hafr Al-Batn, in Northeastern Saudi Arabia. The accident left Moe critically brain-injured and comatose. Saudi Prince Muhammad bin Naif bin Abdul-Aziz Al-Saud, the current Minister of the Interior and nephew of King Abdullah, personally sponsored Moe's medical care and his mother's travel to, and accommodations in Saudi Arabia. This book chronicles years of child and spousal physical, mental and sexual abuse that culminated in abduction, tragedy and hope. Available in Kindle and paperback at Amazon.com and Createspace.com

http://www.amazon.com/dp/B00JUW16XE   https:www.createspace.com/4775674

(Children's fiction/5 stars) **"Mulberry May Belle"**

MULBERRY MAY BELLE is not your average eight year-old girl. With friends like 'Tentacled Ted,' who lives in her closet; 'Mr. Mummy,' who visits with her at night, and a ghostly boy named 'Bill,' Mulberry (along with her step-sister, Lonnie) occupies herself with 'scaring' trains via mulberry stains, and playing games on cemetery plains...Wednesday Addams would LOVE her, and you will too. Available in Kindle and paperback at Amazon.com and Createspace.com

http://www.amazon.com/Mulberry-May-Belle-Marla-Buchanan-ebook/dp/B00KRQ5LUQ/ref=pd_sim_kstore_2?ie=UTF8&refRID=1JWX1RH9C7RYH2MVB11W

https://www.createspace.com/4839356

Everyone knows how to 'kill' a zombie , but do they know how to accurately guess their 'age' based on their appearance and state of decay? This book, written by an author with a B.A. in Anthropology, explains the science of decay (including a "Zombie Timeline of Decay," for reference) in easy to understand language that will help the reader impress their fellow zombie fans with their new-found expertise in zombie anatomy. They'll never watch a zombie movie or T.V. show the same way again!

http://www.amazon.com/dp/B00LCVBPAA https://www.createspace.com/4875643

AUTHOR'S CONTACT INFO:

FACEBOOK

http://www.facebook.com/rescueinarabia

TWITTER

MarlaBuchanan13

AMAZON AUTHOR'S PAGE

http://www.amazon.com/author/marlabuchanan

www.ingramcontent.com/pod-product-compliance
Lightning Source LLC
Chambersburg PA
CBHW060808290526
45792CB00005BA/1574